Zoo ANIMAL FRIENDS™

Michele Wilcox

Packy the Elephant,
page 8

Tian Tian
the Panda,
page 3

Queenie the Koala
& Baby Victoria,
page 14

Peary the
Polar Bear,
page 20

Able the Monkey,
page 6

Ari the Lion,
page 12

Grey the Zebra,
page 10

Sheila the Kangaroo
& Baby Joey,
page 17

Annie's®

A Note From the Designer

I loved designing this book of zoo animals, coming up with the animal ideas and giving them each their own personality. Everyone in my family has a different favorite. I like the monkey best and my husband likes the lion. My grandchildren, of course, want them all!

It was fun to create the clothing and accessories as everything is mix and match. You could easily just make one or two of the animals and then all of the clothes and bags to go along with them.

I have been a knit designer for over 25 years. I love it. I especially enjoy designing animals, so I was very excited to do this book. I hope you enjoy the patterns as much as I do!

Michele Wilcox

Tian Tian the Panda

Gauge
18½ sts and 26½ rows = 4 inches/10cm in St st.

To save time, take time to check gauge.

Pattern Notes
All "adult" animals are the same size and the same gauge. They are all made with the same yarn; the colors and color sequences change.

Head and main body are worked from top down.

Head & Body
Make 2

With MC, cast on 12 sts.

Row 1 (RS): *K1, kfb; rep from * across—18 sts.

Row 2: Purl.

Row 3: *K2, kfb; rep from * across—24 sts.

Row 4: Purl.

Rows 5–22: Continue in St st without further shaping.

Row 23: K2tog across row—12 sts.

Row 24 (WS): Knit (forms neck ridge).

Row 25: Knit.

Row 26: Change to CC and purl across.

Row 27: Kfb across row—24 sts.

Row 28: Purl.

Row 29: *K3, kfb; rep from * across—30 sts.

Row 30: Purl.

Rows 31–34: Work even in St st.

Row 35: Change to MC and knit across.

Rows 36–50: Work even in St st.

Row 51: *K3, k2tog; rep from * across—24 sts.

Row 52: Purl.

Row 53: *K2, k2tog; rep from * across—18 sts.

Row 54: Purl.

Bind off.

Eye Patch
Make 2

With CC, cast on 3 sts.

Row 1 (RS): Kfb in each st across—6 sts.

Row 2: Purl.

Row 3: Knit.

Row 4: Purl.

Row 5: K2tog across row—3 sts.

Row 6: P3tog.

Fasten off and cut yarn, leaving a 12-inch tail to use for sewing to face.

Sew button to center of each eye patch.

Arm
Make 2

With CC, cast on 18 sts.

Rows 1–14: Work even in St st.

Row 15: *K1, k2tog; rep from * across—12 sts.

Row 16: Purl.

Row 17: K2tog across row—6 sts.

Cut yarn, leaving an 18-inch tail.

Using tapestry needle, thread tail through rem sts and pull tight.

Sew underarm seam.

Fill arm with polyester stuffing and sew closed, with underarm seam along one side.

Leg
Make 2

With CC, cast on 21 sts.

Rows 1–14: Work evenly in St st.

Row 15: *K5, k2tog; rep from * across—18 sts.

Row 16: Purl.

Row 17: *K1, k2tog; rep from * across—12 sts.

Row 18: P2tog across row—6 sts.

Cut yarn, leaving an 18-inch tail.

Using tapestry needle, thread tail through rem sts and pull tight.

Sew inner leg seam.

Fill leg with stuffing and sew closed, with inner leg seam along one side.

Snout
With MC, cast on 18 sts.

Row 1 (RS): Knit.

Row 2: Purl.

Row 3: *K1, k2tog; rep from * across—12 sts.

Row 4: Purl.

Row 5: K2tog across row—6 sts.

Row 6: Purl.

Cut yarn, leaving a 12-inch tail.

Using tapestry needle, thread tail through rem sts and pull tight.

Sew snout seam.

Ear
Make 2

With CC, cast on 12 sts.

Row 1 (RS): *K1, kfb; rep from * across—18 sts.

Row 2: Purl.

Rows 3–6: Work evenly in St st.

Row 7: *K1, k2tog; rep from * across—12 sts.

Row 8: *P2tog; rep from * across—6 sts.

Cut yarn, leaving a 12-inch tail.

Using tapestry needle, thread tail through rem sts and pull tight.

Sew side of ear seam.

Finishing
Sew front to back, leaving bottom edge of body open.

Fill head and body with stuffing and sew bottom opening closed.

Sew arms to side seams, starting at neck and matching CC stripe.

Sew legs to bottom of body.

Sew ears to either side of top of head.

Sew eye patches to face.

Fill snout lightly with stuffing and sew to face.

Referring to photo, with CC, embroider nose with satin st and mouth with straight st.

Weave in ends. ●

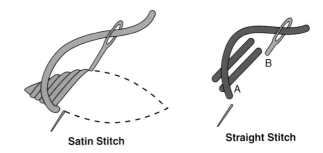

Satin Stitch   **Straight Stitch**

Able the Monkey

Skill Level

◼◻◻◻ EASY

Finished Measurement
11 inches high

Materials
- Premier Deborah Norville Everyday Soft Worsted Yarn (worsted weight; 100% acrylic; 203 yds/113g per skein): 1 skein each terra cotta #1034 (MC) and cappuccino #1035 (CC)
- Size 6 (4mm) needles or size needed to obtain gauge
- Polyester stuffing
- 2 (⅜-inch) buttons
- Tapestry needle
- 5 yds black yarn (Everyday Soft Worsted #1012) or embroidery floss

Gauge
18½ sts and 26½ rows = 4 inches/10cm in St st.

To save time, take time to check gauge.

Pattern Notes
All "adult" animals are the same size and the same gauge. They are all made with the same yarn; the colors and color sequences change.

Head and main body are worked from top down.

Head & Body, Arms & Legs
Make same as for Panda beg on page 3, using MC only.

Sew front to back, leaving bottom edge of body open.

Fill head and body with stuffing and sew bottom opening closed.

Sew arms to side seams, with top of arm just below neck ridge.

Sew legs to bottom of body.

Ear
Make 2

With CC, cast on 8 sts.

Row 1 (RS): Kfb of each st across—16 sts.

Row 2: Purl.

Row 3: *K1, kfb; rep from * across—24 sts.

Row 4: Purl.

Row 5: Knit.

Row 6: Purl.

Rows 7 and 8: Rep Rows 5 and 6.

Row 9: K2tog across row—12 sts.

Row 10: P2tog across row—6 sts.

Cut yarn, leaving a 12-inch tail.

Using tapestry needle, thread tail through rem sts and pull tight.

Sew side of ear seam.

Sew ears in place along either side of head.

Nose
With CC, cast on 30 sts.

Row 1: Knit.

Row 2: Purl.

Row 3: *K3, k2tog; rep from * across—24 sts.

Row 4: Purl.

Row 5: *K2, k2tog; rep from * across—18 sts.

Row 6: Purl.

Row 7: P2tog across row—6 sts.

Cut yarn, leaving a 12-inch tail.

Using tapestry needle, thread tail through rem sts and pull tight.

Sew snout seam.

Sew snout in place on center of face, stuffing lightly before closing.

Referring to photo, with black yarn, embroider mouth with straight st and nostrils with French knots.

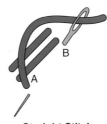
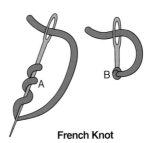

Straight Stitch   French Knot

Sew eyes in place.

Tail
With MC, cast on 12 sts.

Rows 1 (RS)–44: Work in St st.

Row 45: K2tog across row—6 sts.

Cut yarn, leaving an 18-inch tail.

Using tapestry needle, thread tail through rem sts and pull tight.

Sew tail seam, stuffing lightly as you go.

Sew tail in place to lower back of Monkey.

Weave in ends. ●

Packy the Elephant

Skill Level

 EASY

Finished Measurement
11 inches high

Materials
- Premier Deborah Norville Everyday Soft Worsted Yarn (worsted weight; 100% acrylic; 203 yds/113g per skein): 1 skein steel #1024
- Size 6 (4mm) needles or size needed to obtain gauge
- Polyester stuffing
- 2 (⅜-inch) buttons
- Tapestry needle

Gauge
18½ sts and 26½ rows = 4 inches/10cm in St st.

To save time, take time to check gauge.

Pattern Notes
All "adult" animals are the same size and the same gauge. They are all made with the same yarn; the colors and color sequences change.

Head and main body are worked from top down.

Head & Body, Arm & Leg
Make same as for Panda beg on page 3, using one color (steel) only.

Sew front to back, leaving bottom edge of body open.

Fill head and body with stuffing and sew bottom opening closed.

Sew arms to side seams, with top of arm just below neck ridge.

Sew legs to bottom of body.

Ear
Make 2

Note: Row 13 will produce a fold line.

Cast on 8 sts.

Row 1 (RS): Kfb in each st across—16 sts.

Row 2: Purl.

Rows 3–10: Work even in St st.

Row 11: K2tog across row—8 sts.

Rows 12–14: Knit.

Row 15: Kfb in each st across—16 sts.

Row 16: Purl.

Rows 17–24: Work even in St st.

Row 25: K2tog across row—8 sts.

Bind off, leaving a 12-inch tail.

Fold ear in half along fold line and sew side seams.

Sew bottom edges tog (cast-on edge to bound-off edge) and then to either side of head.

Trunk

Cast on 15 sts.

Row 1 (RS): Knit.

Row 2: Purl.

Row 3: *K3, k2tog; rep from * across—12 sts.

Rows 4 and 5: Knit.

Row 6: Purl.

Row 7: *K2, k2tog; rep from * across—9 sts.

Rows 8 and 9: Knit.

Row 10: Purl.

Rows 11–13: Knit.

Rows 14: Purl.

Rows 15–22: Rep [Rows 11–14] twice.

Row 23: [K2tog] twice, k1, [k2tog] twice—5 sts.

Cut yarn, leaving an 18-inch tail.

Using tapestry needle, thread tail through rem sts and pull tight.

Sew trunk seam, stuffing lightly as you go.

Sew trunk in place to face of Elephant.

Sew eyes in place.

Weave in ends. •

Grey the Zebra

Finished Measurement
11 inches high

Materials

- Premier Deborah Norville Everyday Soft Worsted Yarn (worsted weight; 100% acrylic; 203 yds/113g per skein): 1 skein each cream #1002 (MC) and black #1012 (CC)
- Size 6 (4mm) needles or size needed to obtain gauge
- Polyester stuffing
- 2 (⅜-inch) buttons
- Tapestry needle
- 1 yd red embroidery floss

Gauge
18½ sts and 26½ rows = 4 inches/10cm in St st.

To save time, take time to check gauge.

Pattern Notes
All "adult" animals are the same size and the same gauge. They are all made with the same yarn; the colors and color sequences change.

Head and main body are worked from top down.

Head & Body
Make same as for Panda beg on page 3, starting with CC and alternating 2 rows of CC and 2 rows of MC throughout. Carry unused yarn loosely along side of piece.

Arm
Make 2

With CC, cast on 18 sts.

Rows 1–12: Work even in St st, alternating stripes of CC and MC as on head and body.

Change to CC for rem of arm.

Rows 13 and 14: Work even in St st.

Row 15: *K1, k2tog; rep from * across—12 sts.

Row 16: Purl.

Row 17: K2tog across row—6 sts.

Cut yarn, leaving an 18-inch tail.

Using tapestry needle, thread tail through rem sts and pull tight.

Sew underarm seam.

Fill arm with polyester stuffing and sew closed, with underarm seam along one side.

Leg
Make 2

With CC, cast on 21 sts.

Rows 1–12: Work even in St st, alternating stripes of CC and MC as on head and body.

Change to CC for rem of leg.

Rows 13 and 14: Work even in St st.

Row 15: *K5, k2tog; rep from * across—18 sts.

Row 16: Purl.

Row 17: *K1, k2tog; rep from * across—12 sts.

Row 18: P2tog across row—6 sts.

Cut yarn, leaving an 18-inch tail.

Using tapestry needle, thread tail through rem sts and pull tight.

Sew inner leg seam.

Fill leg with stuffing and sew closed, with inner leg seam along one side.

Nose
With CC, cast on 15 sts.

Row 1 (RS): Knit.

Row 2: Purl.

Change to MC.

Row 3: *K4, kfb; rep from * across—18 sts.

Row 4: Purl.

Change to CC for rem of nose.

Rows 5–8: Work even in St st.

Row 9: K2tog across row—9 sts.

Cut yarn, leaving an 18-inch tail.

Using tapestry needle, thread tail through rem sts and pull tight.

Sew bottom of nose seam.

Ear
Make 2

With CC, cast on 3 sts.

Row 1 (RS): Knit.

Row 2: Purl.

Row 3: *K1, kfb; rep from * across—6 sts.

Row 4: Purl.

Row 5: K1, *kfb; rep from * until 1 st rems, k1—10 sts.

Row 6: Purl.

Rows 7–10: Work even in St st.

Bind off.

Fold ear in half lengthwise and sew seam.

Finishing
Matching stripes, sew front to back, leaving bottom edge of body open.

Fill head and body with stuffing and sew bottom opening closed.

Sew arms to side seams, with top of arm just below neck ridge.

Sew legs to bottom of body.

Fill nose with stuffing and sew to face.

Referring to photo, with red embroidery floss, embroider mouth with straight st.

To shape nostrils, using tapestry needle and CC, stitch through nose, back and forth a few times, pulling to indent. Secure ends; cut and hide ends inside of nose.

Straight Stitch

Sew eyes to face.

Mane
Note: *Referring to photo, place mane on head starting at front of top CC section and going halfway down back of head.*

Cut 18 (7-inch) lengths of CC.

Using 2 strands at a time, thread needle with yarn ends even. Starting at top of head, pass needle from right to left through head until a loop has formed. Draw ends of yarn through loop and tighten. Cut loop and remove needle.

Rep for rem fringe down back of head.

Brush and trim.

Weave in ends. ●

Ari the Lion

Finished Measurement

11 inches high

Materials

- Premier Deborah Norville Everyday Soft Worsted Yarn (worsted weight; 100% acrylic; 203 yds/113g per skein): 1 skein each mustard #1028 (MC), cream #1002 (CC1) and black #1012 (CC2)
- Size 6 (4mm) needles or size needed to obtain gauge
- Polyester stuffing
- 2 (⅜-inch) buttons
- Tapestry needle
- 2 yds off-white carpet thread (for whiskers)

Gauge

18½ sts and 26½ rows = 4 inches/10cm in St st.

To save time, take time to check gauge.

Pattern Notes

All "adult" animals are the same size and the same gauge. They are all made with the same yarn; the colors and color sequences change.

Head and main body are worked from top down.

Head & Body, Arm & Leg

Make same as for Panda beg on page 3, using MC only.

Sew front to back, leaving bottom edge of body open.

Fill head and body with stuffing and sew bottom opening closed.

Sew arms to side seams, with top of arm just below neck ridge.

Sew legs to bottom of body.

Ear

Make 2

With MC, cast on 8 sts.

Row 1 (RS): Kfb in each st across—16 sts.

Row 2: Purl.

Row 3: *K1, kfb; rep from * across—24 sts.

Row 4: Purl.

Row 5: Knit.

Row 6: Purl.

Row 7: K2tog across row—12 sts.

Cut yarn, leaving a 12-inch tail.

Using tapestry needle, thread tail through rem sts and pull tight.

Sew side of ear seam.

Sew in place on either side of center top of head.

Snout

With CC1, cast on 5 sts.

Row 1 (RS): Knit.

Row 2: Purl.

Row 3: [K1, kfb] twice, k1—7 sts.

Rows 4–8: Work even in St st.

Change to CC2.

Rows 9–11: Work even in St st.

Row 12: P2tog, p3, p2tog—5 sts.

Row 13: K2tog, k1, k2tog—3 sts.

Cut yarn, leaving a 12-inch tail.

Using tapestry needle, thread tail through rem sts and pull tight.

Sew snout to face, stuffing lightly.

Sew eyes in place.

Referring to photo, with CC2, embroider mouth with straight st.

Straight Stitch

Mane

Note: Referring to photo, place mane on sides and top of head in 2 rows from shoulder to shoulder.

Cut 150 (9-inch) lengths of CC1.

Using 2 strands at a time, thread needle with yarn ends even. Starting at either shoulder, pass needle from right to left through head until a loop has formed. Draw ends of yarn through loop and tighten. Cut loop and remove needle.

Rep for rem fringe across head, working fringe behind ears.

Make a 2nd row close to the first.

Brush to fluff and trim.

Whiskers

Thread needle with 2 strands of carpet thread. Attach same as fringe on either side of snout where CC1 and CC2 meet. Trim.

Weave in ends. •

Queenie the Koala & Baby Victoria

Finished Measurements

Koala: 11 inches high
Baby: 6 inches high

Materials

- Premier Deborah Norville Everyday Soft Worsted Yarn (worsted weight; 100% acrylic; 203 yds/113g per skein): 1 skein caramel #1014 (MC), cream #1002 (CC1) and black #1012 (CC2)
- Size 6 (4mm) needles or size needed to obtain gauge
- Polyester stuffing
- 2 (⅜-inch) buttons
- Tapestry needle

4 MEDIUM

Gauge

18½ sts and 26½ rows = 4 inches/10cm in St st.

To save time, take time to check gauge.

Pattern Notes

All "adult" animals are the same size and the same gauge. They are all made with the same yarn; the colors and color sequences change.

Head and main body are worked from top down.

Koala

Head & Body, Arms & Legs

Make same as for Panda beg on page 3, using MC only.

Sew front to back, leaving bottom edge of body open.

Fill head and body with stuffing and sew bottom opening closed.

Sew arms to side seams, with top of arm just below neck ridge.

Sew legs to bottom of body.

Ear

Make 4

With MC, cast on 8 sts.

Row 1 (WS): Purl.

Row 2: Kfb in each st across—16 sts.

Row 3: Purl.

Row 4: Knit.

Row 5: Purl.

Row 6: K2, k2tog, k8, k2tog, k2—14 sts.

Row 7: Purl.

Row 8: K2, k2tog, k6, k2tog, k2—12 sts.

Row 9: Purl.

Row 10: K2, k2tog, k4, k2tog, k2—10 sts.

Row 11: Purl.

Row 12: K2, [k2tog] 3 times, k2—7 sts.

Bind off.

With RS facing out, sew 2 pieces along sides and top (bound-off) edges tog.

Sew ears in place along either side of top of head.

Ear Fur
Cut 32 (8-inch) lengths of CC1.

Using 2 strands at a time, thread needle making yarns ends even. Starting at top of inner ear, pass needle from right to left, through front of ear until a loop has formed. Draw ends of yarn through loop and tighten. Cut loop and remove needle.

Rep for rem fur, working 4 fur fringes across.

Make a 2nd row close to the first.

Brush to fluff and trim.

Nose
With CC2, cast on 5 sts.

Row 1 (RS): Knit.

Row 2: Purl.

Row 3: Knit.

Row 4: P1, p3tog, p1—3 sts.

Row 5: Knit.

Row 6: P3tog.

Cut yarn, leaving a 12-inch tail.

Referring to photo and using tapestry needle, thread tail and use to sew nose to center of face.

Sew eyes in place.

Baby

Head & Body
Make 2

Beg at top of head, with MC, cast on 4 sts.

Row 1 (RS): Kfb in each st across—8 sts.

Row 2: Purl.

Row 3: Kfb in each st across—16 sts.

Rows 4–14: Work even in St st.

Row 15: K2tog across row—8 sts.

Row 16: Knit (forms neck ridge).

Row 17: Knit.

Row 18: Purl.

Row 19: Kfb in each st across—16 sts.

Rows 20–30: Work even in St st.

Row 31: *K2, k2tog; rep from * across—12 sts.

Row 32: Purl.

Row 33: *K1, k2tog; rep from * across—8 sts.

Row 34: Purl.

Row 35: K2tog across row—4 sts.

Bind off.

Sew front to back, leaving bottom edge of body open.

Fill head and body with stuffing and sew bottom opening closed.

Arms
Make 2

With MC, cast on 10 sts.

Rows 1–8: Starting with a knit row, work in St st.

Row 9: K2tog across row—5 sts.

Cut yarn, leaving a 12-inch tail.

Using tapestry needle, thread tail through rem sts, stuff and then pull tight to close.

Sew underarm seams.

Sew arms to sides of body.

Leg
Make 2

With MC, cast on 12 sts.

Rows 1–8: Starting with a knit row, work in St st.

Row 9: K2tog across row—6 sts.

Row 10: Purl.

Cut yarn, leaving a 12-inch tail.

Using tapestry needle, thread tail through rem sts, stuff and then pull tight to close.

Sew inner leg seams.

Sew legs to bottom of body.

Ear
Make 2

With MC, cast on 8 sts.

Row 1 (RS): Kfb in each st across—16 sts.

Row 2: Purl.

Row 3: Knit.

Row 4: Purl.

Row 5: K2tog across row—8 sts.

Row 6: Purl.

Cut yarn, leaving a 9-inch tail.

Using tapestry needle, thread tail through rem sts and pull tight, gathering last row into a circle.

Sew ears in place along either side of top of head.

Ear Fur
Cut 16 (8-inch) lengths of CC1.

Using 2 strands at a time, thread needle with yarn ends even. Starting at top of inner ear, pass needle from right to left, through front of ear until a loop has formed. Draw ends of yarn

through loop and tighten. Cut loop and remove needle.

Rep for rem fur, working 4 fur fringes across.

Brush to fluff and trim.

Nose
With CC2, cast on 4 sts.

Rows 1–3: Starting with a knit row, work in St st.

Row 4: [P2tog] twice—2 sts.

Cut yarn, leaving a 9-inch tail.

Using tapestry needle, thread tail through rem sts and pull tight.

Sew nose to center of face.

With CC2, embroider eyes with French knots.

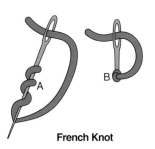

French Knot

Weave in ends. ●

Sheila the Kangaroo & Baby Joey

Finished Measurements
Kangaroo: 11 inches high
Baby: 4½ inches high

Materials
- Premier Deborah Norville Everyday Soft Worsted Yarn (worsted weight; 100% acrylic; 203 yds/113g per skein): 1 skein cappuccino #1035
- Size 6 (4mm) needles or size needed to obtain gauge
- Polyester stuffing
- 2 (⅜-inch) buttons
- Tapestry needle
- 5 yds black yarn (Everyday Soft Worsted #1012) or embroidery floss

Gauge
18½ sts and 26½ rows = 4 inches/10cm in St st.

To save time, take time to check gauge.

Pattern Notes
All "adult" animals are the same size and the same gauge. They are all made with the same yarn; the colors and color sequences change.

Head and main body are worked from top down.

Kangaroo

Head & Body, Arms & Legs
Make same as for Panda beg on page 3 using one color (cappuccino) only.

Sew front to back, leaving bottom edge of body open.

Fill head and body with stuffing and sew bottom opening closed.

Sew arms to side seams, with top of arm just below neck ridge.

Sew legs to bottom of body.

Pouch
Cast on 28 sts.

Rows 1–4: *K2, p2; rep from * across.

Rows 5–20: Starting with a knit row, work even in St st.

Row 21 (RS): K2tog across row—14 sts.

Row 22: Purl.

Bind off.

Pin pouch to body, centering on lower front with bottom (bound-off edge) just above lower body seam. Sew pouch in place along sides and bottom, leaving top (ribbed edge) free.

Ear
Make 2

Cast on 3 sts.

Row 1 (RS): Knit.

Row 2: Purl.

Row 3: Kfb of each st across—6 sts.

Row 4: Purl.

Row 5: K1, [kfb] 4 times, k1—10 sts.

Row 6: Purl.

Row 7: K3, [kfb] 4 times, k3—14 sts.

Row 8: Purl.

Row 9: Knit.

Row 10: Purl.

Row 11: K5, [kfb] 4 times, k5—18 sts.

Rows 12–16: Work even in St st.

Row 17: K2tog across row—9 sts.

Cut yarn, leaving a 12-inch tail.

Using tapestry needle, thread tail through rem sts and pull tight, gathering last row into a circle.

Sew ears in place along either side of top of head.

Snout
Cast on 5 sts.

Row 1 (RS): Kfb of each st across—10 sts.

Row 2: Purl.

Row 3: *K1, kfb; rep from * across—15 sts.

Row 4: Purl.

Row 5: *K2, kfb; rep from * across—20 sts.

Row 6: Purl.

Row 7: Knit.

Cut yarn, leaving a 12-inch tail.

Using tapestry needle, thread tail through rem sts and pull tight.

Sew snout seam.

Sew snout in place on center of face, stuffing lightly before closing.

Referring to photo, with black yarn or floss, embroider nose with satin st and mouth with straight st.

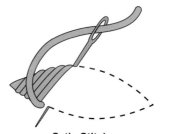

Satin Stitch   Straight Stitch

Sew eyes in place.

Tail
Cast on 28 sts.

Rows 1–4: Starting with a knit row, work in St st.

Row 5: *K5, k2tog; rep from * across—24 sts.

Rows 6–10: Work even in St st.

Row 11: *K4, k2tog; rep from * across—20 sts.

Rows 12–16: Work even in St st.

Row 17: *K3, k2tog; rep from * across—16 sts.

Rows 18–22: Work even in St st.

Row 23: *K2, k2tog; rep from * across—12 sts.

Row 24: Purl.

Cut yarn, leaving an 18-inch tail.

Using tapestry needle, thread tail through rem sts and pull tight.

Sew tail seam, stuffing lightly as you go.

Sew tail in place to lower back of Kangaroo.

Baby

Head & Body
Beg at bottom of body, cast on 6 sts.

Row 1: Kfb of each st across—12 sts.

Row 2: Purl.

Row 3: *K1, kfb; rep from * across—18 sts.

Row 4: Purl.

Row 5: *K2, kfb; rep from * across—24 sts.

Rows 6–10: Work even in St st.

Row 11: K2tog across row—12 sts.

Row 12: Knit (forms neck ridge).

Row 13: Knit.

Row 14: Purl.

Row 15: Kfb of each st across—24 sts.

Rows 16–18: Work even in St st.

Row 19: K6, [k2tog] 6 times, k6—18 sts.

Rows 20–22: Work even in St st.

Row 23: K2tog across row—9 sts.

Row 24: [P2tog] 4 times, P1—5 sts.

Cut yarn, leaving a 12-inch tail.

Using tapestry needle, thread tail through rem sts and pull tight.

Sew back of body and head seam, stuffing lightly before closing.

Referring to photo, with black yarn or floss, embroider eyes with French knots, nose with satin st and mouth with straight st.

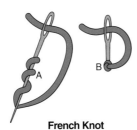

French Knot

Arm
Make 2

Cast on 8 sts.

Rows 1–6: Starting with a knit row, work in St st.

Cut yarn, leaving a 12-inch tail.

Using tapestry needle, thread tail through rem sts, stuff and then pull tight to close.

Sew underarm seams.

Sew arms to sides of body.

Leg
Make 2

Make same as for arms.

Sew legs to bottom of body.

Ear
Make 2

Cast on 3 sts.

Row 1 (RS): Knit.

Row 2: Purl.

Row 3: Kfb of each st across—6 sts.

Row 4: Purl.

Row 5: K1, [kfb] 4 times, k1—10 sts.

Row 6: Purl.

Row 7: Knit.

Row 8: P2tog across row—5 sts.

Cut yarn, leaving a 9-inch tail.

Using tapestry needle, thread tail through rem sts and pull tight, gathering last row into a circle.

Sew ears in place along either side of top of head.

Weave in ends. ●

Peary the Polar Bear

Skill Level

 EASY

Finished Measurement
11 inches high

Materials
- Premier Deborah Norville Everyday Soft Worsted Yarn (worsted weight; 100% acrylic; 203 yds/113g per skein): 1 skein snow white #1001
- Size 6 (4mm) needles or size needed to obtain gauge
- Polyester stuffing
- 2 (⅜-inch) buttons
- Tapestry needle
- 5 yds black yarn (Everyday Soft Worsted #1012) or embroidery floss

Gauge
18½ sts and 26½ rows = 4 inches/10cm in St st.

To save time, take time to check gauge.

Pattern Notes
All "adult" animals are the same size and the same gauge. They are all made with the same yarn; the colors and color sequences change.

Head and main body are worked from top down.

Head & Body, Arm & Leg
Make same as for Panda beg on page 3, using one color (snow white) only.

Sew front to back, leaving bottom edge of body open.

Fill head and body with stuffing and sew bottom opening closed.

Sew arms to side seams, with top of arm just below neck ridge.

Sew legs to bottom of body.

Snout
Cast on 15 sts.

Row 1 (RS): Knit.

Row 2: Purl.

Row 3: *K1, k2tog; rep from * across—10 sts.

Row 4: Purl.

Row 5: K2tog across row—5 sts.

Row 6: Purl.

Cut yarn, leaving a 12-inch tail.

Using tapestry needle, thread tail through rem sts and pull tight.

Sew snout seam.

Fill snout lightly with stuffing and sew to face.

Referring to photo, with black yarn or floss, embroider nose with satin st and mouth with straight st.

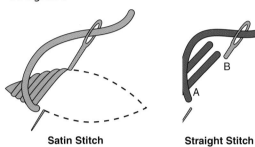

Satin Stitch   **Straight Stitch**

Sew button eyes in place.

Ear
Make 2

Cast on 6 sts.

Row 1 (RS): Knit.

Row 2: Purl.

Row 3: K2tog across row—3 sts.

Row 4: Purl.

Row 5: Kfb across row—6 sts.

Row 6: Purl.

Row 7: Knit.

Bind off.

Cut yarn, leaving a 12-inch tail.

Fold in half with RS facing out and sew side seams.

Sew bottom of ear (cast-on and bound-off edges) to either side of top of head.

Weave in ends. •

Accessories

Sweater

Skill Level

■■□□ EASY

Finished Measurements
Chest: 14 inches
Length: 4 inches

Materials
- Premier Deborah Norville Everyday Soft Worsted Yarn (worsted weight; 100% acrylic; 203 yds/113g per skein): 1 skein baby pink #1006
- Size 6 (4mm) needles or size needed to obtain gauge
- 1 (½-inch) heart-shaped button

Gauge
18½ sts and 26½ rows = 4 inches/10cm in St st.

To save time, take time to check gauge.

Back
Cast on 34 sts.

Row 1 (RS): *K2, p2; rep from * until 2 sts rem, k2.

Row 2: *P2, k2; rep from * until 2 sts rem, p2.

Rows 3–10: Rep [Rows 1 and 2] 4 times.

Rows 11–22: Starting with a knit row, work in St st.

Row 23: *K4, k2tog; rep from * until 4 sts rem, k4—29 sts.

Row 24: Purl.

Rows 25 and 26: Bind off 4 sts, knit to end—21 sts.

Row 27: K2tog, k1, p2, [k2, p2] 4 times—20 sts.

Rows 28–30: *K2, p2; rep from * across.

Bind off.

Right Front
Cast on 20 sts.

Row 1 (RS): K4, *k2, p2; rep from * across.

Row 2: *K2, p2; rep from * until 4 sts rem, k4.

Rows 3–10: Rep [Rows 1 and 2] 4 times.

Row 11: Knit.

Row 12: P16, k4.

Rows 13–22: Rep [Rows 11 and 12] 5 times.

Row 23: K7, k2tog, [k3, k2tog] 2 times, k1—17 sts.

Row 24: P13, k4.

Row 25: Knit.

Row 26: Bind off 4 sts, p9, k4—13 sts.

Row 27: K4, k2tog, k1, p2, k2, p2—12 sts.

Row 28 (buttonhole row): [K2, p2] twice, k1, yo, k2tog, k2.

Row 29: K4, [k2, p2] 2 times.

Row 30: Rep Row 28.

Bind off.

Left Front
Cast on 20 sts.

Row 1 (RS): *K2, p2; rep from * until 4 sts rem, k4.

Row 2: K4, *k2, p2; rep from * across.

Rows 3–10: Rep [Rows 1 and 2] 4 times.

Row 11: Knit.

Row 12: K4, p16.

Rows 13–22: Rep [Rows 11 and 12] 5 times.

Row 23: K1, [k2tog, k3] twice, k2tog, k7—17 sts.

Row 24: K4, p13.

Row 25: Bind off 4 sts, k12—13 sts.

Row 26: K4, p9.

Row 27: K2tog, k1, p2, k2, p2, k4—12 sts.

Row 28: K4, [k2, p2] twice.

Row 29: [K2, p2] twice, k4.

Row 30: Rep Row 28.

Bind off.

Sleeve
Make 2

Cast on 20 sts.

Rows 1–5: Knit.

Row 6 (WS): Purl.

Rows 7–10: Starting with a knit row, work in St st.

Bind off.

Finishing
Sew shoulder and neck trim seams.

Center tops of sleeves to shoulder and sew in place.

Sew side and underarm seams.

Sew button to left front opposite buttonhole.

Weave in ends.

Stocking Cap

Skill Level
◼◼◻◻ EASY

Finished Measurements
Circumference: 12 inches
Length: 13 inches

Materials
- Premier Deborah Norville Everyday Soft Worsted Yarn (worsted weight; 100% acrylic; 203 yds/113g per skein): 1 skein each electric green #1038 (MC) and cornflower #1018 (CC)
- Size 6 (4mm) needles or size needed to obtain gauge

Gauge
18½ sts and 26½ rows = 4 inches/10cm in St st.

To save time, take time to check gauge.

Pattern Stitch
Stripe Sequence

*2 rows CC, 2 rows MC; rep from * for sequence.

Hat
With (MC), cast on 52 sts.

Rows 1–6: *K2, p2; rep from * across.

Row 7: Knit.

Row 8: Purl.

Change to CC and begin Stripe Sequence.

Rows 9–18: Rep [Rows 7 and 8] 5 times.

Row 19: With MC, *K11, k2tog; rep from * across—48 sts.

Rows 20–22: Continuing in pat, work even in St st.

Row 23: *K6, k2tog; rep from * across—42 sts.

Rows 24–26: Work even in pat.

Row 27: *K5, k2tog; rep from * across—36 sts.

Rows 28–30: Work even in pat.

Row 31: *K4, k2tog; rep from * across—30 sts.

Rows 32–36: Work even in pat.

Row 37: *K3, k2tog; rep from * across—24 sts.

Rows 38–46: Work even in pat.

Row 47: *K2, k2tog; rep from * across—18 sts.

Rows 48–66: Work even in pat.

Row 67: *K1, k2tog; rep from * across—12 sts.

Rows 68–80: Work even in pat.

Row 81: K2tog across row—6 sts.

Row 82: Purl.

Cut yarn, leaving a 30-inch tail.

Using tapestry needle, thread tail through rem sts and pull tight.

Sew back of hat seam.

Weave in ends.

With MC, make a 1½-inch pompom.

Sew pompom to pointed tip of hat.

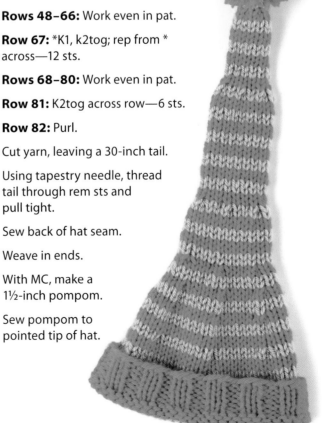

Scarf

Skill Level
 EASY

Finished Measurements
Length: 15 inches
Width: 1½ inches

Materials
- Premier Deborah Norville Everyday Soft Worsted Yarn (worsted weight; 100% acrylic; 203 yds/113g per skein): 1 skein scarlet #1025

- Size 6 (4mm) needles or size needed to obtain gauge

Gauge
18½ sts and 26½ rows = 4 inches/10cm in St st.

To save time, take time to check gauge.

Scarf
Cast on 7 sts.

Row 1: *K1, p1; rep from * to last st, k1.

Rep Row 1 until scarf measures 15 inches.

Bind off.

Weave in ends.

Bag

Skill Level
 EASY

Finished Measurement
Length with Strap: 8 inches

Materials
- Premier Deborah Norville Everyday Soft Worsted Yarn (worsted weight; 100% acrylic; 203 yds/113g per skein): 1 skein scarlet #1025
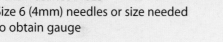
- Size 6 (4mm) needles or size needed to obtain gauge

Gauge
18½ sts and 26½ rows = 4 inches/10cm in St st.

To save time, take time to check gauge.

Bag
Cast on 40 sts.

Rows 1–22: *K2, p2; rep from * across.

Row 23: *K2tog, p2tog; rep from * across—20 sts.

Row 24: *K1, p1; rep from * across.

Row 25: Rep Row 24.

Row 26: *K2tog across row—10 sts.

Cut yarn, leaving an 18-inch tail.

Using tapestry needle, thread tail through rem sts and pull tight.

Sew bag seam.

Strap
Cast on 6 sts.

Rows 1–38: *K1, p1; rep from * across.

Bind off.

Sew short ends of strap to either side of top of bag.

Weave in ends.

Poncho

Skill Level
■■□□ EASY

Finished Measurements
Circumference: 24 inches
Length: 3½ inches

Materials
- Premier Deborah Norville Everyday Soft Worsted Yarn (worsted weight; 100% acrylic; 203 yds/113g per skein): 1 skein bittersweet #1022
- Size 6 (4mm) needles or size needed to obtain gauge

Gauge
18½ sts and 26½ rows = 4 inches/10cm in St st.

To save time, take time to check gauge.

Poncho
Make 2

Cast on 26 sts.

Row 1 (RS): *K2, p2; rep from * to last 2 sts, k2.

Row 2: *P2, k2; rep from * to last 2 sts, p2.

Rows 3–8: Rep [Rows 1 and 2] 3 times.

Row 9: Kfb of each st across—52 sts.

Rows 10–18: Starting with a purl (WS) row, work even in St st.

Rows 19–24: Knit.

Bind off.

Sew poncho side seams.

Weave in ends.

Vest

Skill Level
■■□□ EASY

Finished Measurements
Chest: 10½ inches
Length: 4 inches

Materials
- Premier Deborah Norville Everyday Soft Worsted Yarn (worsted weight; 100% acrylic; 203 yds/113g per skein): 1 skein each electric green #1038 (MC) and scarlet #1025 (CC)
- Size 6 (4mm) needles or size needed to obtain gauge

Gauge
18½ sts and 26½ rows = 4 inches/10cm in St st.

To save time, take time to check gauge.

Pattern Stitch
Stripe Sequence
*4 rows CC, 2 rows MC; rep from * for sequence.

Vest
Make 2

Note: Main body pieces are worked side to side.

With MC, cast on 16 sts.

Rows 1–5: *K2, p2; rep from * across.

Row 6: Purl.

Change to CC and beg Stripe Sequence.

Rows 7–42: Start with a knit row and work in St st.

Rows 43–46: Continuing with MC, *k2, p2; rep from * across.

Bind off in ribbing.

Bottom Edge
With RS facing, using MC, pick up and knit 34 sts from one side of vest pieces, between Rows 7 and 40.

Row 1 (WS): *K2, p2; rep from * to last 2 sts, k2.

Row 2: *P2, k2; rep from * to last 2 sts, p2.

Rows 3–8: Rep [Rows 1 and 2] 3 times.

Bind off in ribbing.

Neck Edge
With RS facing, using MC, pick up and knit 34 sts from other side of vest pieces, between Rows 7 and 40.

Row 1 (WS): *K2, p2; rep from * to last 2 sts, k2.

Row 2: *P2, k2; rep from * to last 2 sts, p2.

Rows 3 and 4: Rep Rows 1 and 2.

Bind off in ribbing.

Sew ribbing tog at neck, shoulders, underarm and side seams.

Weave in ends.

Shorts

Finished Measurements
Waist: 7 inches
Length: 4 inches

Materials
- Premier Deborah Norville Everyday Soft Worsted Yarn (worsted weight; 100% acrylic; 203 yds/113g per skein): 1 skein each royal blue #1009 (MC) and electric green #1038 (CC)
- Size 6 (4mm) needles or size needed to obtain gauge
- 2 (⅝-inch) buttons

Gauge
18½ sts and 26½ rows = 4 inches/10cm in St st.

To save time, take time to check gauge.

Shorts
Make 2

Note: Shorts pieces are worked from the waist down.

With MC, cast on 32 sts.

Rows 1–6: *K1, p1; rep from * across.

Row 7 (RS): Knit.

Row 8: Purl.

Row 9: *K7, kfb; rep from * across—36 sts.

Rows 10–20: Starting with a purl row, work even in St st.

Rows 21–28: Knit.

Bind off kwise.

Fold each piece in half and sew Rows 20–28 (garter section) tog to form bottom of shorts.

Sew front edges tog from crotch to top of waist.

Sew back edges tog from crotch to top of waist, leaving a 1½-inch opening in center of back seam for tail.

Suspender
Make 2

With CC, cast on 5 sts.

Rows 1–62: Knit.

Bind off.

Referring to photo, sew one short end of each suspender to top of waist at the center of each back piece. Crisscross suspenders and sew opposite short ends to front of waist at center of each front piece.

Sew decorative buttons in place on front ends of suspenders.

Weave in ends.

Tote

Finished Measurement
Length: 7 inches, including strap

Materials
- Premier Deborah Norville Everyday Soft Worsted Yarn (worsted weight; 100% acrylic; 203yds/113g per skein): 1 skein electric green #1038
- Size 6 (4mm) needles or size needed to obtain gauge

Gauge

18½ sts and 26½ rows = 4 inches/10cm in St st.

To save time, take time to check gauge.

Tote
Cast on 16 sts.

Rows 1–4: *K1, p1; rep from * across.

Row 5: *K1, kfb; rep from * across—24 sts.

Rows 6–14: Starting with a purl row, work even in St st.

Row 15 (RS): K2tog across row—12 sts.

Rows 16–18: Knit (forms folding lines).

Row 19: Kfb of each st across—24 sts.

Rows 20–28: Starting with a purl row, work even in St st.

Row 29: *K1, k2tog; rep from * across row—16 sts.

Rows 30–33: *K1, p1; rep from * across.

Bind off in ribbing.

Fold piece in half, matching ribbed edges together.

Sew side seams.

Strap
Cast on 40 sts.

Row 1: Knit.

Bind off kwise.

Sew short ends of strap to either side of top of tote.

Weave in ends. ●

General Information

Abbreviations & Symbols

[ ] work instructions within brackets as many times as directed

( ) work instructions within parentheses in the place directed

** repeat instructions following the asterisks as directed

* repeat instructions following the single asterisk as directed

" inch(es)

approx approximately
beg begin/begins/beginning
CC contrasting color
ch chain stitch
cm centimeter(s)
cn cable needle
dec(s) decrease/decreases/ decreasing
dpn(s) double-point needle(s)
g gram(s)
inc(s) increase/increases/ increasing

k knit
k2tog knit 2 stitches together
kfb knit in front and back
kwise knitwise
LH left hand
m meter(s)
M1 make one stitch
MC main color
mm millimeter(s)
oz ounce(s)
p purl
p2tog purl 2 stitches together
pat(s) pattern(s)
pm place marker
psso pass slipped stitch over
pwise purlwise
rem remain/remains/remaining
rep(s) repeat(s)
rev St st reverse stockinette stitch
RH right hand
rnd(s) rounds
RS right side

skp slip, knit, pass slipped stitch over—1 stitch decreased
sk2p slip 1, knit 2 together, pass slipped stitch over the knit 2 together—2 stitches decreased
sl slip
sl 1 kwise slip 1 knitwise
sl 1 pwise slip 1 purlwise
sl st slip stitch(es)
ssk slip, slip, knit these 2 stitches together—a decrease
st(s) stitch(es)
St st stockinette stitch
tbl through back loop(s)
tog together
WS wrong side
wyib with yarn in back
wyif with yarn in front
yd(s) yard(s)
yfwd yarn forward
yo (yo's) yarn over(s)

Skill Levels

BEGINNER

Beginner projects for first-time knitters using basic stitches. Minimal shaping.

EASY

Easy projects using basic stitches, repetitive stitch patterns, simple color changes and simple shaping and finishing.

INTERMEDIATE

Intermediate projects with a variety of stitches, mid-level shaping and finishing.

EXPERIENCED

Experienced projects using advanced techniques and stitches, detailed shaping and refined finishing.

Knitting Basics

Long-Tail Cast-On

Leaving an end about an inch long for each stitch to be cast on, make a slip knot on the right needle.

Place the thumb and index finger of your left hand between the yarn ends with the long yarn end over your thumb, and the strand from the skein over your index finger. Close your other fingers over the strands to hold them against your palm. Spread your thumb and index fingers apart and draw the yarn into a "V."

Place the needle in front of the strand around your thumb and bring it underneath this strand. Carry the needle over and under the strand on your index finger.

Draw through loop on thumb.

Drop the loop from your thumb and draw up the strand to form a stitch on the needle.

Repeat until you have cast on the number of stitches indicated in the pattern. Remember to count the beginning slip knot as a stitch.

Purl (P)

With yarn in front, insert tip of right needle from back to front through next stitch on the left needle.

Wrap yarn around the right needle counterclockwise. With right needle, draw yarn back through the stitch.

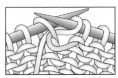

Slide the stitch off the left needle.

The new stitch is on the right needle.

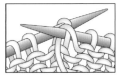

Knit (K)

Insert tip of right needle from front to back in next stitch on left needle.

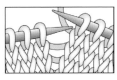

Wrap yarn under and over the tip of the right needle.

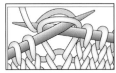

Pull yarn loop through the stitch with right needle point.

Slide the stitch off the left needle. The new stitch is on the right needle.

Bind-Off

Binding Off (Knit)

Knit first two stitches on left needle. Insert tip of left needle into first stitch worked on

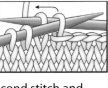

right needle and pull it over the second stitch and completely off the needle.

Knit the next stitch and repeat. When one stitch remains on right needle, cut yarn and draw tail through last stitch to fasten off.

Binding Off (Purl)

Purl first two stitches on left needle. Insert tip of left needle into first stitch worked on right needle and pull it over the

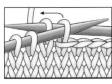

second stitch and completely off the needle.

Purl the next stitch and repeat. When one stitch remains on right needle, cut yarn and draw tail through last stitch to fasten off.

Increase (inc)

Two Stitches in One Stitch

Knit in Front & Back of Stitch (kfb)

Knit the next stitch in the usual manner, but don't remove the stitch from the left needle. Place right needle behind left needle and knit again into the back of the same stitch. Slip original stitch off left needle.

Purl in Front & Back of Stitch (pfb)

Purl the next stitch in the usual manner, but don't remove the stitch from the left needle. Place right needle behind left needle and purl again into the back of the same stitch. Slip original stitch off left needle.

Decrease (Dec)

Knit 2 Together (K2tog)

Insert right needle through next two stitches on left needle as to knit. Knit these two stitches as one.

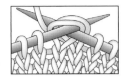

Purl 2 Together (P2tog)

Insert right needle through next two stitches on left needle as to purl. Purl these two stitches as one.

Jogless Join

When changing colors, knit the entire first round with the new color, stopping at the beginning-of-round stitch marker. Slip the first stitch of the second round of the new color purlwise, and then continue knitting around.

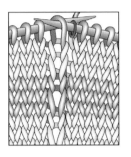

Meet the Designer

Michele has been designing knitted items for many years; there is nothing she would rather do. Her grandmother taught her to knit when she was 5 or 6 years old. She loved it right from the start.

Up until the age of 19, she didn't know much more than the knit stitch, but then became determined to increase her knitting skills and make mittens for her fiancé so he would throw away the pair someone else had knit for him. She then taught herself to crochet and loves to design for both crafts.

Her designs have been published by Annie's, *Better Homes and Gardens*, Coats & Clark, Universal Yarn and Herrschners.

Special Thanks

Special thanks to Premier Yarns for supplying the Deborah Norville Everyday Soft Worsted Yarn for this book.

Premier Yarns
Premier Yarns Customer Service
2800 Hoover Road
Stevens Point, WI 54481
(888) 458-3588
www.premieryarns.com

Photo Index

3

14

6

8

10

12

17

20

Annie's® *Zoo Animal Friends* is published by Annie's, 306 East Parr Road, Berne, IN 46711. Printed in USA. Copyright © 2013 Annie's. All rights reserved. This publication may not be reproduced in part or in whole without written permission from the publisher.

RETAIL STORES: If you would like to carry this pattern book or any other Annie's publications, visit AnniesWSL.com.

Every effort has been made to ensure that the instructions in this pattern book are complete and accurate. We cannot, however, take responsibility for human error, typographical mistakes or variations in individual work. Please visit AnniesCustomerCare.com to check for pattern updates.

978-1-59635-737-2
2 3 4 5 6 7 8 9